CW00411323

Beethoven
Library of Piano Works

Volume I: Dances, Songs and Studies

Compiled and Edited by
Donald and Delayna Beattie

Art Design: Thais Yanes

© 2001 BELWIN-MILLS PUBLISHING CORP. (ASCAP)
All Rights Administered by WARNER BROS. PUBLICATIONS U.S. INC.
All Rights Reserved

Any duplication, adaptation or arrangement of the compositions
contained in this collection requires the written consent of the Publisher.
No part of this book may be photocopied or reproduced in any way without permission.
Unauthorized uses are an infringement of the U.S. Copyright Act and are punishable by law.

9631A

999   M1118

Contents

Preface

Out of a world of silence came forth the triumphant and joyous Symphony No. 9. With works like the Ninth Symphony's *Ode to Joy, Für Elise*, the "Moonlight" piano sonata, Symphony No. 5, and music of his later years that carry listeners to a higher place, Beethoven demonstrated that, indeed, one man can make the world a better place.

Aside from Beethoven's familiar pieces, each day of his life he looked inside and brought forth music compositions that express what we all experience and know to be true. In the face of some of life's greatest difficulties, Beethoven gave his life to music and, in turn, gave the world one of its greatest treasures. All of us who love music and who cherish the gift of life come to know Beethoven as our teacher. Within the musical notes of his compositions, which he thought of as poetry and his peers deemed "tone paintings," Beethoven serves as a wise and faithful guide on life's journey. For those of us who teach, we are privileged to bring Beethoven into the lives of our students so that their journeys maintain a joyful course. As Beethoven himself said, "He who understands my music can never know unhappiness again."

This library is designed to accompany each young piano student for a lifetime. Beginning with Beethoven's lesser-known yet extraordinary beginning piano works, the library advances progressively through his repertoire with CD performance recordings included in each volume. Equally important are the writings entitled *Beethoven as Our Teacher*, artwork and photographic reproductions that bring his life before our eyes, and performance notes for practice, interpretation, and teaching.

At times, Beethoven is portrayed as an eternally angry composer. All who enjoy this library will come to know and cherish Beethoven as a living hero. Through his music, he is a man who profoundly expressed his heartaches and sorrows while never losing sight of the gift and joy of life. By playing his music, we are consoled and at the same time transported to regions of the heart and soul that teach some of life's greatest lessons. No matter the age, the time, the place, or the person, Beethoven's music reaches the heart. He accomplished his goal with an inscription found on the manuscript of the *Missa Solemnis*: "From the heart, may it go to the heart." Joseph Karl Stieler's 1820 painting of Beethoven was selected to adorn the covers of this library.

Our love of Beethoven began long ago as children and continued with the founding of the Beethoven Society for Pianists in 1984. Beethoven's music and message has brought us together for countless festivals to celebrate the gifts and friendship of children, parents, families, teachers, and some of the greatest artists of our time. With this library, it is our dream to expand the world of those, especially children, who enjoy, learn, and experience Beethoven's beautiful music and to enlighten others of his deep desire for peace, joy, and friendship throughout the world.

Donald and Delayna Beattie

About the Compositions
German Dance in F Major (1811–1812)

This little-known piece of Beethoven's was found as a sketch in one of his manuscripts. It is a charming example of all that Beethoven can compose with a three-note motive and I and V7 harmony. As much as we love Beethoven, he did write little that is accessible to the younger player. For this dance and the studies that follow, we include an example of how Beethoven's easier piano works can be adapted for younger players. Beethoven would not discourage teachers and students from creating musical adaptations of his early pieces as students grow and mature with his music.

In beginning the piece, one finds an opening right-hand three-note motive of A B♭ C, a second motive of E F G and three-note motive that follow within a five-note F major scale position, and a left-hand accompaniment based on a harmonic progression that moves I V7 V7 I four times. One finds how truly remarkable it is that even Beethoven's greatest music depends on continual use of simple tonic I and dominant V7 harmonies. From the beginning of this book, we begin a wonderful journey with Beethoven. When ready, students can play the second presentation of this Dance exactly as notated by Beethoven.

Studies in C Major and B-flat Major

A month before his passing, Beethoven remarked to a friend, "It was my wish to write many another thing. I wanted to compose the Tenth Symphony, and then a Requiem as well, and even a piano method. This last I would have done in a way different from that in which others have written them." Unfortunately, time did not allow Beethoven the opportunity for these compositions and projects. However, these two piano pieces that he intended for inclusion in his method survive.

As with the German Dance No. 1, we suggest simplification that does not disturb the beauty of the music but more readily allows playing by younger pianists. In place of the bass notes that begin left-hand playing in the many measures of the Study in C Major, substitute the two- and three-note playing that follows. This omits left-hand skips that have their own challenge. Therefore, the left-hand would begin playing middle C and E above. The piece itself is a marvelous example of music making that begins and ends in major while going to music making in the relative minor in the center. As for the Study in B-flat Major, left-hand notes can be repeated rather than played as a broken octave, and in the variation that follows, the right hand can play single notes rather than octaves. This piece evokes a great change of mood as the music transforms from major and minor.

Russian Folksong in A Minor, "Beautiful Minka," Opus 107, No. 7
Little Russian Folksong in B Major, Opus 107, No. 3
"St. Patrick's Day" in F Major, Opus 107, No. 4

George Thomson of Scotland commissioned Beethoven to write folksong arrangements that Beethoven composed from 1817–1818. This writing was to influence Beethoven's later instrumental works as echoes of his folksong arrangements. Examples are found in his piano sonatas Opus 109 and 110, in some bagatelles and ecossaises, and in his string quartets, Opus 130 and 132. If interested, teachers and students who seek out the complete Opus 107 will find that these folksongs serve as themes for many variations. In fact, the original work proposes performance with either solo piano or as accompaniment to flute or violin. Since the variations have a great range of difficulty, they are not included here, but they remind us of Beethoven's devotion to and great skill with the art of improvisation, the art of making music.

All three folksong arrangements appear as they do in Beethoven's autograph. There are far fewer editorial indications than often appear in publications of these pieces. We are always best reminded about our need to interpret music in hearing J. S. Bach's reply to a student asking why the great composer didn't indicate more editorial markings in his compositions: "Any good musician will know what to do." In our experience, we all become good musicians as we study the score in search of expressive playing. As for *St. Patrick's Day*, this appears in publication least often and is a beautiful piano composition to end this volume. Like other simplifications proposed, the left-hand playing of this piece could be changed to dotted quarter notes from quarter- and eighth-note patterns to ease the playing for practice on the way to playing as written.

Romance in B Minor, WoO1, No. 4

From a supplement to the Breitkopf & Hartel nineteenth-century edition of Beethoven's complete works, we read, "Count Ferdinand Waldstein commissioned Beethoven to write a ballet. This Knights' ballet was written in 1790 when Beethoven was 19. It was performed in Bonn in old German costumes by the local nobility on a carnival Sunday, March 6, 1791. The ballet was made up of eight short pieces." The Romance in B Minor is number four from that set of eight pieces. The appearance of G-sharp in the first eight measures suggests a different scale. With B as tonic and a key signature in the opening measures of three sharps, Beethoven is writing in a B Dorian scale. Dorian is always found from the second degree of a major scale. Looking far ahead to Beethoven's Tenth Symphony, which he had planned to compose in "the old church modes" as well as his Opus 132 string quartet with a slow movement entitled "Hymn of Thanksgiving to the Deity in Lydian," this Romance is an important starting point for Beethoven.

The WoO numbers are a result of the twentieth-century Beethoven scholarship of Georg Kinsky and Hans Halm. They cataloged Beethoven's unpublished works and issued them each a WoO number reflecting the German words *werke ohne opus* (work without opus.)

Ecossaise for Military Music in G Major, WoO23

Ecossaise is generally termed "a French word meaning Scotch." The Ecossaise was a popular dance in 2/4 time, usually used for beginning and ending an evening of dancing. Chopin and Schubert also wrote these and subtitled them "Scotch Dances." *Ecossaise for Military Music* was Beethoven's original title of this work. It was composed in 1810 and published by Carl Czerny after Beethoven's death. Not unlike the very first German Dance of this collection, Beethoven writes so creatively with I and V7 harmony. Only in measure 14 is there a change of harmony to IV. Perhaps Beethoven alone could have named I, IV, and V7 "Primary Triads"!

German Dances
In F Major, WoO42, No. 1
In A Major, WoO42, No. 4
In F Major, WoO42, No. 3
In G Major, WoO42, No. 6

We know that Beethoven composed these pieces, drawn from a collection of six pieces, between the years 1795–1796. We also know that he originally composed these works for violin and piano. Whether performed as piano solo or with a violinist, these dances in major keys evoke very cheery and joyful feelings. These compositions were written in the early years of Beethoven's life in Vienna. Having moved to Vienna in 1792 from Bonn, Beethoven was looking to establish himself as a composer and performer. As we will see in Volume II of this series, these dances date from about the same time that Beethoven was receiving commissions to write dances for masked balls in Vienna. Although those pieces were composed for small chamber orchestra, they come down to us as solo piano pieces thanks to Beethoven, Carl Czerny, and other colleagues who made piano transcriptions.

In all four of these pieces, harmonic analysis will reveal much about Beethoven's writing. In short, he is always able to do much with little. To paraphrase, Beethoven was said to have remarked to Anton Schindler that one must learn the fundamentals of harmony between the ages of seven and eleven. This way, as one reaches emotional maturity, he or she will do so with command of the expressive language of music. We have always joked that for those of us who did not reach this point by the age of eleven, we must continue study between the hours of seven and eleven for life!

Beethoven as Our Teacher

Beethoven and the *Ode to Joy*

Ferdinand Schiller's text from the final movement of Symphony No. 9

Beethoven's Birthplace
Pencil drawing by R. Beissel (1889)

O friends, not these strains—
Rather let us sing
More pleasing songs, and more joyous.

Joy, thou gleaming spark divine,
Daughter of Elysium,
Drunk with ardor, we draw near,
Goddess, to thy shrine.

Thy magic unites again
What custom sternly drew apart;
All mankind become brothers
Beneath thy gentle hovering wing.

He whose happy fortune grants him
Friend to have and friend to be,
Who has won a noble woman,
Let him join in our rejoicing!

Yes—even were it one heart only
Beating for him in the world!
But if he's never known this, let him
Weeping steal from out our ranks.

Joy is drawn by every creature
From the breast of Nature;
All men good and all men evil
Walk upon her rose-strewn path.

Kisses gave she and the ripe grape,
A good friend, trusty to the last;
Even the worm can feel pleasure,
And the Seraph stands before God.

Glad as suns that He hurtles
Through the vast spaces of heaven,
Pursue your pathway, brothers;
Be joyful as a hero in victory.

Millions, be you embraced!
For the universe, the kiss!
Brothers—above the canopy of stars
A loving Father surely dwells.

Millions, do you fall upon your knees?
Do you sense the Creator, world!
Seek Him above the canopy of stars!
Surely He dwells above the stars.

In Seldon Rodman's book, *The Heart of Beethoven*, the author wrote, "Beethoven had had a poem of Schiller in mind for some such dimly foreseen eventuality ever since he grew up in Bonn. Sketches of the setting date from 1794, 1798, 1811, and 1822 . . . its key line 'All mankind shall be as brothers' summed up succinctly Beethoven's ideal of social destiny . . . the chorale rises to its most dizzying heights as human brotherhood expands to cover the universe: 'Seek Him beyond the canopy of Heaven! He must dwell above the stars.'" During the composition of Symphony No. 9, in a letter to Archduke Rudolph dated July 1, 1823, Beethoven wrote, "I thank Him who is above the stars, that I am beginning to use my eyes again."

Young Beethoven's Music Studies

Christian Gottlob Neefe's (Nay-fe) influence on the young Beethoven was major and of lasting proportions. A man of learning and culture, he introduced Ludwig not only to the great musical classics, but the literary ones as well—Shakespeare, Goethe, Schiller, and the ancients of Greece and Rome. [1]

From the pen of Neefe, dated March 2, 1783: "Louis van Beethoven, son of the tenor singer mentioned, a boy of eleven years and of most promising talent. [Beethoven would have actually been twelve years old in March 1783. He was born in 1770 and, while there is some uncertainty as to the exact date of his birth, his birthday is celebrated December 16.] He plays the clavier very skillfully and with power, reads at sight very well, and—to put it in a nutshell—he plays chiefly *The Well-Tempered Clavier* of Sebastian Bach, which Herr Neefe put into his hands. Whoever knows this collection of preludes and fugues in all the keys—which might almost be called the *ne plus ultra* of our art—will know what this means.

"So far as his duties permitted, Herr Neefe has also given Beethoven instruction in thorough-bass. He is now training him in composition and for his encouragement has had nine variations for the pianoforte, written on a march—by Ernst Christoph Dressler—engraved at Mannheim. This youthful genius is deserving of help to enable him to travel. He would surely become a second Wolfgang Amadeus Mozart were he to continue as he has begun."

In 1788, Beethoven had the opportunity to play for Mozart at the time of Beethoven's first visit to Vienna. Mozart was impressed and said that Beethoven "would make a great noise [music] in the world." Due to the failing health of his parents, Beethoven returned home to Bonn, Germany. Shortly thereafter, Beethoven's mother passed. Although he had a troubling childhood with his father, who was quite cruel to young Beethoven, Ludwig had always been fond of his mother. By the time Beethoven returned to Vienna in 1792, Mozart had passed (1756–1791). Beethoven did go on to music studies with Joseph Haydn and other notable teachers of the day.

1) From the book, *Famous Pianists & Their Technique*, by Reginald Gerig.

Beethoven's Love of Nature During His Early Years

Young Ferdinand Ries reported that "at times, at 8:00 in the morning, after breakfast, Beethoven would say, 'Let us first take a short walk.' We went and frequently did not return until 3:00 or 4:00 that afternoon, having made a meal in some village."

Ignaz von Seyfried wrote, "Friends who dropped by observed Beethoven wandering the fields, as he always did, or composing industriously at his desk. Every year, Beethoven spent the summer months in the country, where under skies of azure blue, he liked best to compose, and composed most successfully. . . . No sooner did he cross the city boundary and find himself among blossoming fields, where gentle zephyrs set the green corn swaying like waves, amid the jubilant song of fluttering larks, celebrating the longed-for coming of lovely spring with trills of raptured greeting, then his genius awoke; thoughts began to traverse his mind, were spun out, ranged in order and noted down in lead pencil."

Beethoven – 1802

Louis Schlosser remarked that "In nature's open, Beethoven's creative powers drew their richest nourishment among the hills and the heavily leaved woods, and where ideas, as he expressed himself, flowed to him in quantity." Sir George Grove recorded a tradition that Beethoven refused to take possession of an engaged lodging because there were no trees near the house: "How is this? Where are your trees?" said Beethoven. "We have none," said the landlord. Beethoven replied, "Then the house won't do for me. I love a tree more than a man."

Beethoven's Piano Playing and Improvisations

The experience of hearing Beethoven improvise was not easily forgotten. The effect was still a vivid memory when Carl Czerny wrote the following description in 1852, a quarter of a century after Beethoven's death: "His improvisation was most brilliant and striking. In whatever company he might chance to be, he knew how to produce such an effect upon every hearer that frequently not an eye remained dry, while many would break out into loud sobs; for there was something wonderful in his expression in addition to the beauty and originality of his ideas and his spirited style of rendering them."

Czerny went on to say, "No one equaled Beethoven in rapidity of scales, double trills, skips—when playing, his demeanor was masterfully quiet, noble and beautiful, without the slightest grimace. Beethoven's performance of slow and sustained passages produced an almost magical effect upon every listener and, so far as I know, was never surpassed." Czerny also realized that both Beethoven's playing and his compositions were far ahead of this time.

Beethoven and the Language of Music

In the house of Prince Lichnowsky, a Hungarian count once laid before Beethoven a difficult composition by Bach, in manuscript, which Beethoven performed with great readiness at sight. One day a musician by the name of Forster brought Beethoven a quartet, which he had copied out only that morning. In the second part of the first movement, the cellist left. Beethoven stood up and, while continuing to play his piano part, sang the bass accompaniment.

To a friend who expressed his wonder at this thorough knowledge, Beethoven said, smiling, "So the bass part had to be, else the author understood nothing of composition." Whereupon the author remarked that Beethoven had played the piano part at presto, which he had never seen before, so fast that it would have been impossible to see the single notes. "That is not necessary," replied Beethoven. "If you read rapidly, you may not see nor heed them, if you only know the language."

Manuscript of the Piano Sonata in G minor, Op. 111 (1822)
First movement, from bar 87

Beethoven on Piano Teaching

In a letter to Carl Czerny in Vienna dated 1817, Beethoven wrote concerning his nephew Karl's piano lessons with Czerny: "Please be as patient as possible with our Karl, even though at present he may not be making as much progress as you and I would like. If you are not patient, he will do even less well, because (although he must not know this), owing to the unsatisfactory timetable for his lessons, he is being unduly strained. Unfortunately, nothing can be done about that for the time being. Treat him therefore, so far as possible, with affection, but be firm with him. Then there will be a greater chance of success in spite of these really unfavourable circumstances where Karl is concerned.

"In regard to his playing for you, as soon as he has learnt the right fingering and can play a piece in correct time and the notes too, more or less accurately, then please check him only about his interpretation; and when he has reached that point, don't let him stop playing for the sake of minor mistakes, but point them out to him when he has finished playing the piece. Although I have done very little teaching, yet I have always followed this method. It soon produces musicians which, after all, is one of the chief aims of the art."

In a letter dated January 7, 1820, Beethoven wrote: "I know no more sacred duty than to rear and educate a child."

Beethoven's Interpretive Vocabulary

Carl Czerny taught his student Theodore Leschetizky much about Beethoven's manner of freely interpreting his own sonatas. Czerny taught that Beethoven should be rendered with freedom of delivery and depth of feeling. A pedantic, inelastic interpretation of the master made Czerny wild. Czerny's vocabulary of character—words to describe the effect Beethoven's works have if played correctly—is extensive. The following list, taken from Czerny's *Piano School,* is by no means complete, yet it gives an idea of the richness of this "interpretive vocabulary."

unruly	serious	tragic	teasing
weighty	fantastic	humorous	pathetic
lulling	firm	intimate	bewitching
determined	fleeting	complaining	religious
brilliant	joyous	strong	roaring
singing	pious	noisy	peaceful
capriciously	tender	lively	touching
chorale-like	witty	light	gentle
delicate	good-natured	charming	jocose
dramatic	powerful	virile	flattering
exalted	sparkling	marked	dejected
simple	expressively	melancholy	speaking
elegant	graceful	merry	stormy
mournful	shrill	murmuring	agitated
energetic	grand	mischievous	profound
resolute	serene	naïve	dreamy
lofty	heroic	unaffected	sensitive

Manuscript of the "Moonlight" Sonata in C-sharp minor, Op. 27, No. 2 (1801)
Beginning of the last movement

Beethoven and His Symphony No. 9

The following story was told to Sir George Grove exactly as written by Madame Sabatier-Ungher in the end gallery of the Crystal Palace Concert Room during her visit to London in 1869: "At the actual first performance of Beethoven's Symphony No. 9 on May 7, 1824, a great deal of emotion was naturally enough visible in the orchestra; and we hear of such eminent players as Mayseder and Bohm even weeping. At the close of the performance an incident occurred which must have brought the tears of many an eye in the room.

"Beethoven, though placed in the midst of this confluence of music, heard nothing of it at all and was not even sensible of the applause of the audience at the end of his great work, but continued standing with his back to the audience, and beating the time, till Fraulein Ungher, who had sung the contralto part, turned him, or induced him to turn round and face the people, who were still clapping their hands, and giving way to the greatest demonstrations of pleasure.

"Beethoven's turning round and the sudden conviction thereby forced on everybody that he had not done so before because he could not hear what was going on, acted like an electric shock on all present, and a volcanic explosion of sympathy and admiration followed, which was repeated again and again and seemed as if it would never end."

In Martin Cooper's book, *Beethoven: The Last Decade*, the author wrote, "Under what influences, in exactly what labour of the imagination and the spirit that innocent introductory flourish [of the first movement of the 9th] swelled and burgeoned, like an acorn swelling into an oak tree, it is impossible to say; but it is hard to resist the feeling that the uniquely indeterminate yet pregnant atmosphere of the introductory bars has some extra-musical affinity. We may never know . . . the exact nature of that . . . extra-musical origin, but Beethoven himself gives us a warrant for divining its presence."

The London German with whom Beethoven got on so famously in 1824, J. A. Stumpff, reported Beethoven as saying, "When I contemplate in wonderment the firmament and the host of luminous bodies which we call worlds and suns, eternally revolving within its boundaries, my spirit soars beyond these stars, many millions of miles away towards the fountain from which all created work springs and from which all new creation must still flow." Beethoven's Ninth Symphony gives hope eternal to all who hear and perform it.

1a. GERMAN DANCE IN F MAJOR[1]

(1811-1812)

LUDWIG VAN BEETHOVEN

1) This musical adaptation of Beethoven's *German Dance No. 1b*, offers
   one example of score simplification for the benefit of younger pianists.
2) Fingering 123 may be best for the finger dexterity of children playing these three-note motives.
   A 345 fingering has the advantage of shifting hand positions from five-note major scales from F and C.
   Choosing 234 may also be of value with the somewhat equal length of the fingers.

1b. GERMAN DANCE IN F MAJOR

(1811-1812)

LUDWIG VAN BEETHOVEN

2. STUDY IN C MAJOR

LUDWIG VAN BEETHOVEN

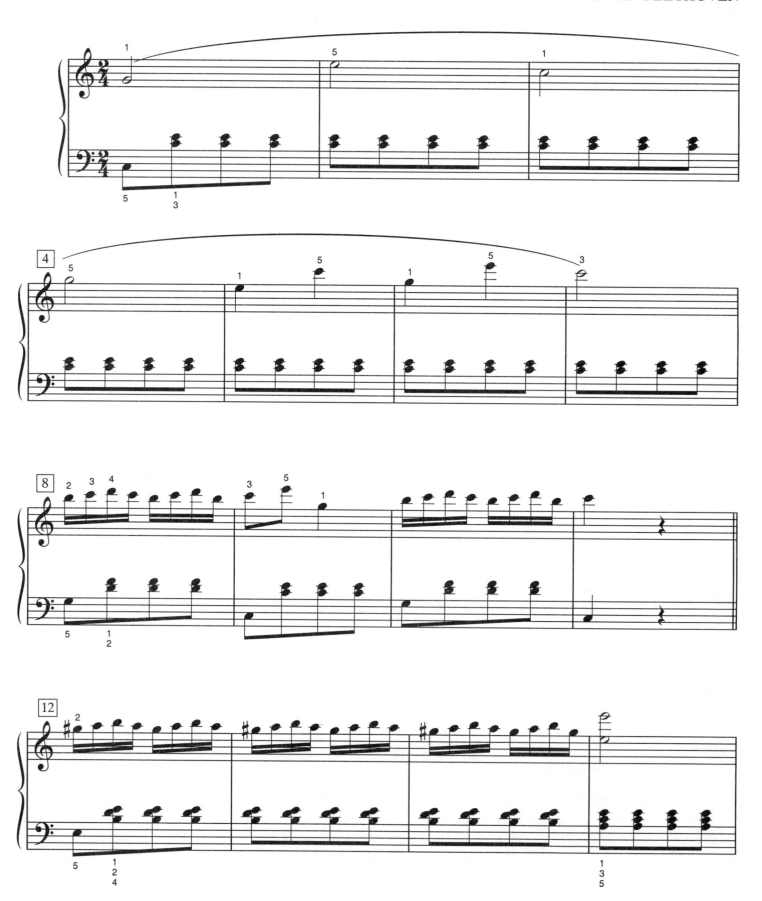

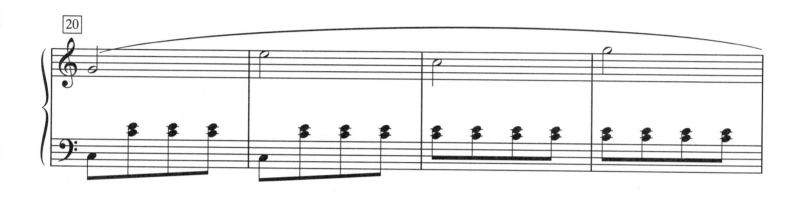

3. RUSSIAN FOLKSONG IN A MINOR "BEAUTIFUL MINKA"

Opus 107, No. 7

LUDWIG VAN BEETHOVEN

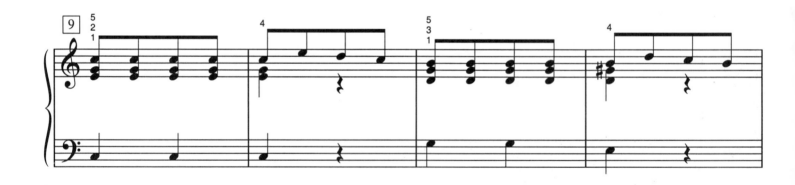

4. LITTLE RUSSIAN FOLKSONG IN G MAJOR

Opus 107, No. 3

LUDWIG VAN BEETHOVEN

5. STUDY IN B-FLAT MAJOR

LUDWIG VAN BEETHOVEN

Variation

D.C. al Fine

6. ROMANCE

(1790, from the *Ritterballet*)
WoO1, No. 4

LUDWIG VAN BEETHOVEN

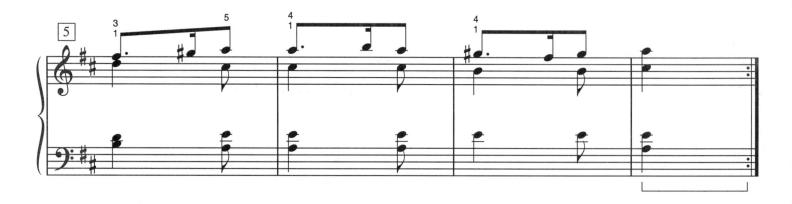

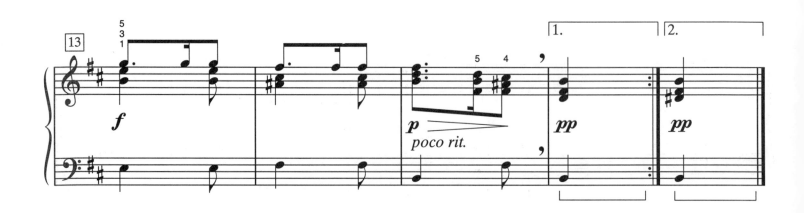

7. "ECOSSAISE FOR MILITARY MUSIC" IN G MAJOR

WoO23

LUDWIG VAN BEETHOVEN

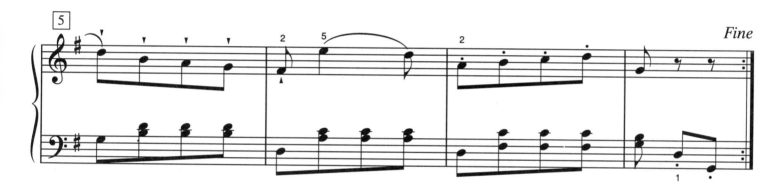

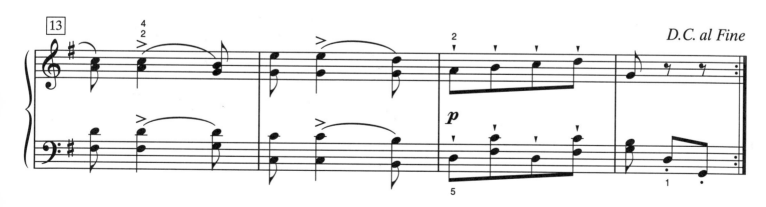

8. GERMAN DANCE IN F MAJOR

WoO42, No. 1

LUDWIG VAN BEETHOVEN

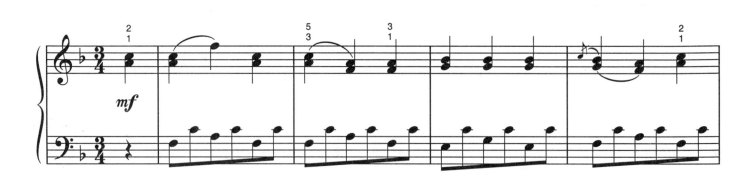

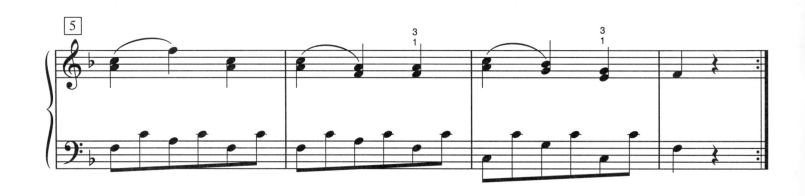

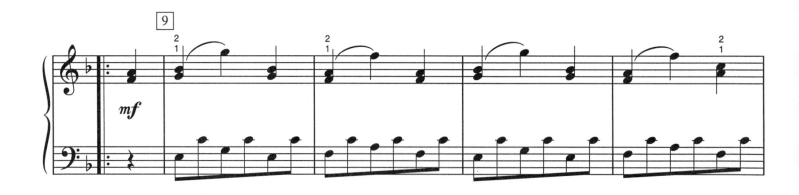

9. GERMAN DANCE IN A MAJOR

WoO42, No. 4

LUDWIG VAN BEETHOVEN

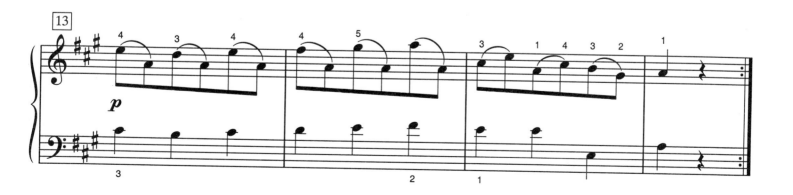

ELM01043CD

10. GERMAN DANCE IN F MAJOR

WoO42, No. 3

LUDWIG VAN BEETHOVEN

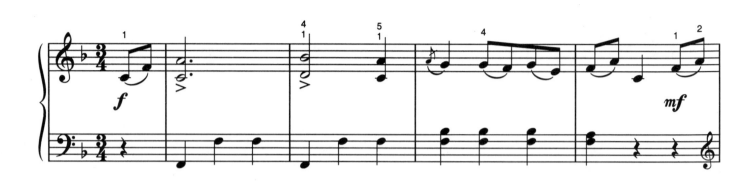

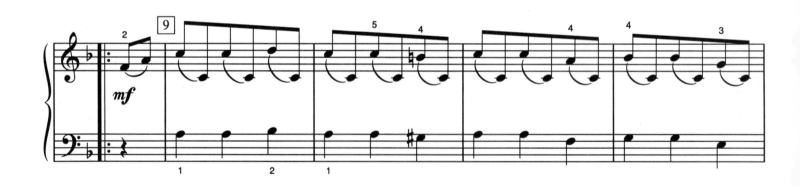

11. GERMAN DANCE IN G MAJOR

WoO42, No. 6

LUDWIG VAN BEETHOVEN

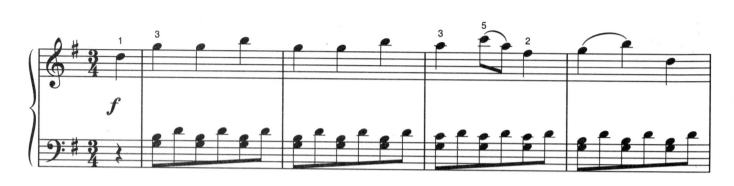

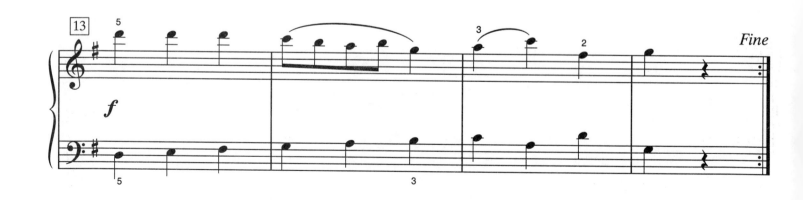

12. "ST. PATRICK'S DAY" IN F MAJOR

Opus 107, No. 4

LUDWIG VAN BEETHOVEN

Allegretto scherzando